# HOW IS IT MADE?
# PAPER

by Erica Donner

# Ideas for Parents and Teachers

Pogo Books let children practice reading informational text while introducing them to nonfiction features such as headings, labels, sidebars, maps, and diagrams, as well as a table of contents, glossary, and index.

Carefully leveled text with a strong photo match offers early fluent readers the support they need to succeed.

## Before Reading

- "Walk" through the book and point out the various nonfiction features. Ask the student what purpose each feature serves.
- Look at the glossary together. Read and discuss the words.

## Read the Book

- Have the child read the book independently.
- Invite him or her to list questions that arise from reading.

## After Reading

- Discuss the child's questions. Talk about how he or she might find answers to those questions.
- Prompt the child to think more. Ask: You can fold it. You can draw on it. You can write a story. What's your favorite way to use paper?

Pogo Books are published by Jump!
5357 Penn Avenue South
Minneapolis, MN 55419
www.jumplibrary.com

Library of Congress Cataloging-in-Publication Data

Names: Donner, Erica, author.
Title: Paper / by Erica Donner.
Description: Minneapolis, MN: Jump!, Inc. 2016.
Series: How is it made? | Includes index.
Identifiers: LCCN 2016040208 (print)
LCCN 2016040675 (ebook)
ISBN 9781620315699 (hardcover: alk. paper)
ISBN 9781620316092 (pbk.)
ISBN 9781624965173 (ebook)
Subjects: LCSH: Paper—Juvenile literature.
Papermaking—Juvenile literature.
Classification: LCC TS1105.5 .D66 2016 (print)
LCC TS1105.5 (ebook) | DDC 676—dc23
LC record available at https://lccn.loc.gov/2016040208

Editor: Jenny Fretland VanVoorst
Designer: Leah Sanders
Photo Researcher: Leah Sanders

Photo Credits: All photos by Shutterstock except:
Alamy, 6-7, 8, 12-13; Getty, 4, 14-15; iStock, 9;
SuperStock, 10-11, 16, 18-19.

Printed in the United States of America at
Corporate Graphics in North Mankato, Minnesota.

# TABLE OF CONTENTS

**CHAPTER 1**
Tree . . . . . . . . . . . . . . . . . . . . . . . . . . . . 4

**CHAPTER 2**
Pulp . . . . . . . . . . . . . . . . . . . . . . . . . . . . 8

**CHAPTER 3**
Paper . . . . . . . . . . . . . . . . . . . . . . . . . . 16

**ACTIVITIES & TOOLS**
Try This! . . . . . . . . . . . . . . . . . . . . . . . 22
Glossary . . . . . . . . . . . . . . . . . . . . . . . . 23
Index . . . . . . . . . . . . . . . . . . . . . . . . . . . 24
To Learn More . . . . . . . . . . . . . . . . . . . 24

# CHAPTER 1

## TREE

Take a sheet of paper. Rip it in half. Now crumple up the pieces. It's hard to believe something you can destroy so easily was once a tall, strong tree.

About 95 percent of all paper comes from trees. Trees used for paper are grown just like any other crop. When they are ready, they are cut down. They are sent to a paper mill.

At the mill, the trees are cut into logs. A machine removes the bark. Then the logs are fed through a **chipper**. It makes wood chips. They are about the size of corn flakes.

**DID YOU KNOW?**

The process for making paper was invented in China in the second century CE. All paper was made one sheet at a time until 1798.

# CHAPTER 2

· · · · · · · · · · · · · · · · · · · · · · · · · · · · · · · · · ·

# PULP

Wood is made of **fibers** of a material called **cellulose**. To become paper, the fibers must be separated. How?

fibers

First, the wood chips are combined with water and chemicals. They are cooked under pressure in a machine called a **digester**.

paper mill

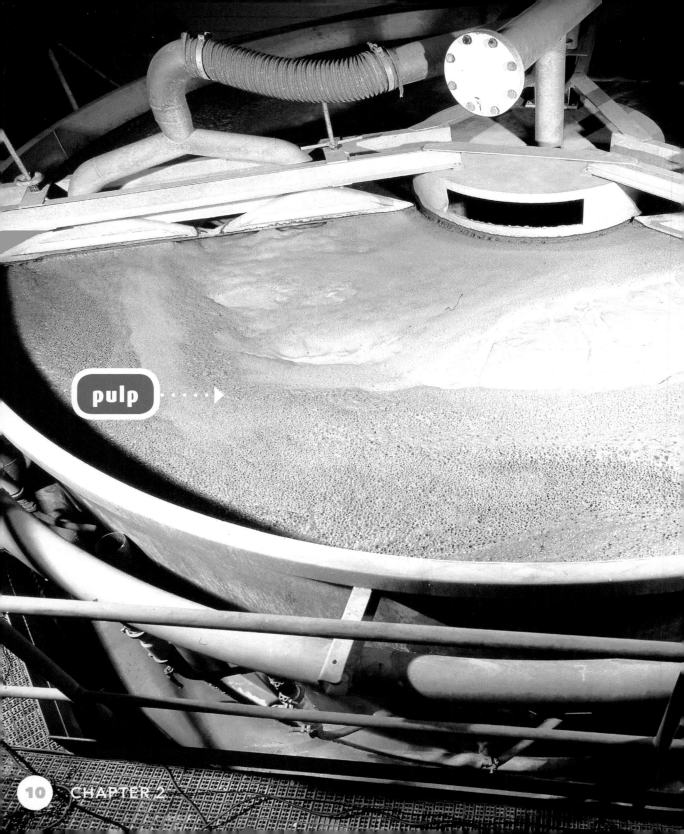

pulp ·····▶

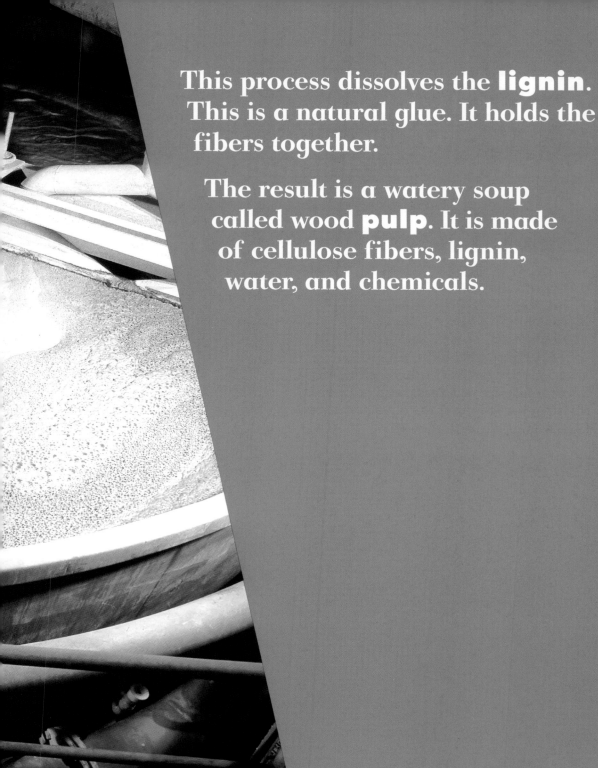

This process dissolves the **lignin**. This is a natural glue. It holds the fibers together.

The result is a watery soup called wood **pulp**. It is made of cellulose fibers, lignin, water, and chemicals.

The pulp is cleaned. It is **bleached**. Then it is turned to slush in a machine called a **beater**. Dyes and **coatings** are mixed in.

## DID YOU KNOW?

In the United States 40 percent of all used paper is recovered for **recycling**. Each time paper is recycled, the fibers get shorter. Shorter fibers make less durable papers. So most recycled papers have some new fibers mixed in with the old.

pulp sprayer

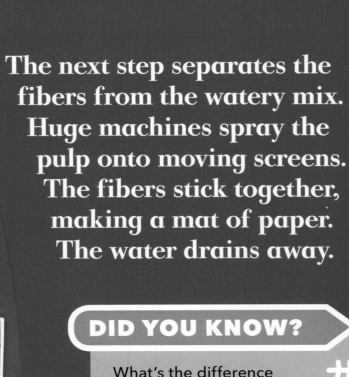

The next step separates the fibers from the watery mix. Huge machines spray the pulp onto moving screens. The fibers stick together, making a mat of paper. The water drains away.

**DID YOU KNOW?**

What's the difference between paper and cloth? To make paper, fibers are pressed together. To make cloth, they are **woven**. This makes cloth a stronger material. You can easily rip a piece of paper. But it's much harder to rip a piece of cloth.

# CHAPTER 3

## PAPER

The paper is squeezed between large rollers. This removes most of the remaining water. It also smooths the paper. It creates a uniform thickness.

A final pass through heated rollers dries the paper.

The paper is then wound into large rolls. They can be 30 feet (9 meters) wide!

A **slitter** cuts the paper into smaller rolls. These rolls are sent off to be made into different kinds of paper.

**DID YOU KNOW?**

Some large machines can produce over 1,000 miles (1,600 kilometers) of paper a day.

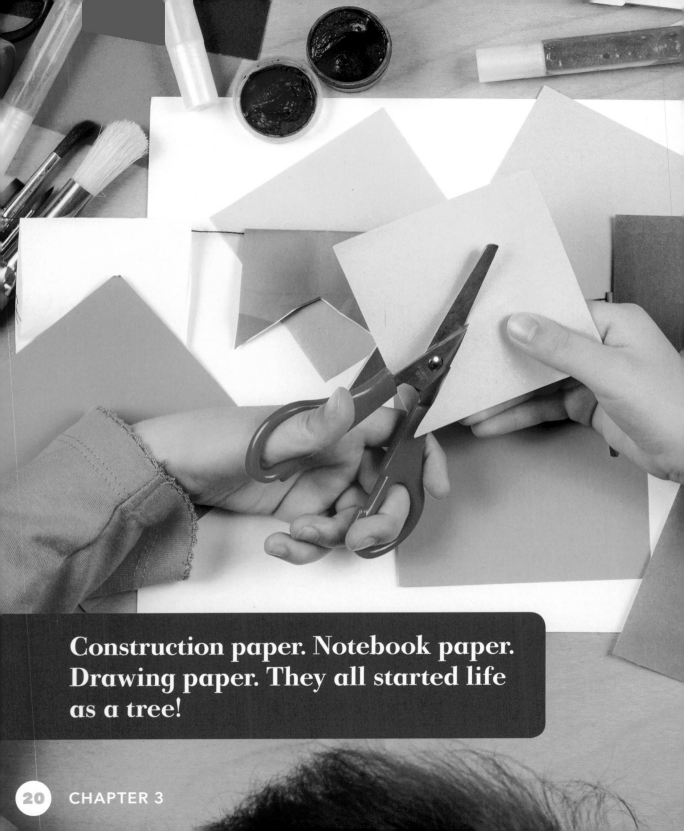

Construction paper. Notebook paper. Drawing paper. They all started life as a tree!

# TAKE A LOOK!

How does a tree become paper?

**Harvesting**

**Pulping**

**Rolling**

**Chipping**

**Spraying**

**Cutting**

# ACTIVITIES & TOOLS

## PAPER STRENGTH TESTING

Not all papers are equally durable. See how different finishes and fiber combinations stack up with this strength test.

**What You Need:**

- various papers, such as recycled notebook paper, non-recycled notebook paper, newspaper, magazine paper, and printer paper
- water
- weights, such as coins or other small objects of uniform weight

① **First, make sure papers are all the same size. Cut them to match, if necessary.**

② **Choose a piece of paper and hold it between both hands. Have a friend help by putting small weights on the paper one at a time. Record the type of paper and how much weight the paper can hold before it rips.**

③ **Now repeat the process with each remaining paper.**

④ **Now wet each piece of paper and repeat the test. Use the same amount of water for each piece of paper, and give it time to absorb.**

⑤ **Look at your results. Which paper was the most durable? Which was the least?**

⑥ **Now think about what each paper is designed for. Is the paper's strength equal to its purpose?**

**beater:** A machine that further liquefies wood pulp.

**bleached:** Treated to remove color.

**cellulose:** The fiber that makes up the cell wall of plants and is used to make paper.

**chipper:** A machine that chips logs into tiny pieces.

**coatings:** Materials added to paper to smooth or roughen the finish or to make it more sturdy.

**digester:** The machine that turns wood chips into wood pulp by pressure-cooking them with water and chemicals.

**fibers:** Long, thin threads of material.

**lignin:** The natural glue that holds cellulose fibers together to form wood.

**pulp:** A soupy mixture made of water, chemicals, lignin, and cellulose.

**recycling:** Processing in order to regain materials for use.

**slitter:** A machine that cuts large rolls of paper into smaller rolls.

**woven:** Laced together.

# INDEX

beater 12

cellulose 8, 11

chemicals 9, 11

China 7

chipper 7, 21

cloth 15

coatings 12

cutting 5, 7, 18, 21

digester 9

drying 17

dyes 12

fibers 8, 11, 12, 15

lignin 11

logs 7

mill 5, 7

pulp 11, 12, 15, 21

recycling 12

rolling 16, 17, 21

rolls 18

screens 15

slitter 18

spraying 15, 21

trees 4, 5, 7, 20, 21

water 9, 11, 15, 16

wood 7, 8, 9, 11

wood chips 7, 9

# TO LEARN MORE

Learning more is as easy as 1, 2, 3.

1) Go to www.factsurfer.com

2) Enter "paper" into the search box.

3) Click the "Surf" button to see a list of websites.

With factsurfer, finding more information is just a click away.

# MORMOR MOVES IN

To Oskar's Mormor and Farmor—
both of them inspirations and
neither of them the least bit grumpy.
—S.N.F.

For my grandma Robertine Dextrase de Bézier,
who lived almost one hundred years.
—L.A.L

Text copyright © 2004 Susin Nielsen-Fernlund

Illustrations copyright © 2004 Louise-Andrée Laliberté

**National Library of Canada Cataloguing in Publication Data**

Nielsen-Fernlund, Susin, 1964-
Mormor moves in / written by Susin Nielsen-Fernlund ; illustrated by Louise-Andrée Laliberté.

ISBN 1-55143-291-9

I. Laliberté, Louise-Andrée  II. Title.

PS8577.I37M67 2004             jC813'.54             C2004-902448-5

First published in the United States 2004

**Library of Congress Control Number:** 2004105775

**Summary:** Astrid and her grandma both learn that another's loss can be as great as her own.

Orca Book Publishers gratefully acknowledges the support for its
publishing programs provided by the following agencies:
the Government of Canada through the Book Publishing
Industry Development Program (BPIDP),
the Canada Council for the Arts, and the British Columbia Arts Council.

Design by Lynn O'Rourke
Scanning: Island Graphics, Victoria
Printed and bound in China

Orca Book Publishers                    Orca Book Publishers
Box 5626 Stn. B                         PO Box 468
Victoria, BC  Canada                    Custer, WA   USA
V8R 6S4                                 98240-0468

# MORMOR
# MOVES IN

*Story by* Susin Nielsen-Fernlund
*Illustrations by* Louise-Andrée Laliberté

Astrid Svensson was five and three-quarters. She had one goldfish, two missing teeth and lots of friends. But her best friend of all was Björn. Astrid had known Björn since the day she was born.

If she was scared to climb the ladder to her tree house, Björn helped her feel brave. If there was a monster under her bed, Björn shooed it away.

Astrid and Björn were a team.

One day, Astrid's mom and dad sat her down. "Your morfar in Sweden has died," they told her. "Your mormor is coming to stay with us."

Astrid had only met her Swedish grandparents twice in her whole life.

"Mormor can play house with us," she said to Björn that night in bed. "And pirates. And store. This will be fun."

But when Mormor arrived, she didn't
want to play.
"*Nej, nej*. Not now, *lilla flicka*," she'd say,
mixing Swedish with English. "I'm busy."
Mormor didn't look busy.
"Maybe this will be fun
later on," Astrid whispered
to Björn.

But at supper, things got worse.
"A teddy bear with his own plate of food?"
Mormor clucked. "How wasteful."
"I eat his food when he gets full," Astrid explained.
"Humph," Mormor said.

The next day, Mormor shouted
at Astrid and Björn while
they played in the tree house.
"Do not put that thing in your
mouth, young lady! It is *smutsig*
—filthy!"

"This," Astrid whispered to
Björn, "will never be fun."

"When is she leaving?" Astrid asked her
mom that night.

"She isn't," her mom replied. "Give her
time, dear. She's not herself."

The next evening, Mormor set the table.
"Where did Morfar go exactly?" Astrid asked.
"To heaven," said her father.
Astrid looked at Mormor. "Then why don't you
go there too?"
Astrid didn't understand why she was sent to her room.

That night, her parents gave her a talk.

"Mormor can't join Morfar, Astrid. He's dead."

"Then I wish she'd die too," Astrid said.

Her mom's eyes got watery and red. "You have to be patient with Mormor," she said.

"You're named after her, you know," her father added. "Her first name is Astrid too."

The next morning, Astrid told her parents that from now on she would be known as "Penelope."

When she got to school, Astrid couldn't find Björn. She searched for him on the walk home. She searched for him all over the house. But Björn was nowhere to be found.

"He was a dirty old *sak*," Mormor said. "It is for the best."

"It is not for the best!" Astrid cried. "I loved him! And you're just a mean old poop!"

This time, Astrid did not wait to be sent to her room.

All week, Astrid was miserable.

Then one day, Mormor saw a bear
that looked exactly like Björn,
except newer and cleaner.

She had an idea.

"Look what I found,"
Mormor said to Astrid
one afternoon.
　"Björn! You found him!
Thank you, Mormor!"

Astrid threw her arms around Mormor. Mormor hugged her back.

"Oh, Björn," Astrid whispered, "it's so good to have you back."

Two Björns?
But how?
What had Mormor done?

Astrid marched to Mormor's door. She
stopped. From inside she heard a noise.
Was Mormor crying?

Astrid thought for a moment.
Then she stepped inside.

"You won't believe
what I found," she said.
"It's Björn's cousin,
Bartholomew. He
wondered if he could
stay with you."

Mormor smiled. "Bartholomew," she said, looking him right in the eye, "I would be delighted."

"You miss Morfar like I missed Björn," Astrid said.

Mormor nodded. Then she said, "Would you like to help me make *pepparkakor*?"

Astrid smiled. "Gingerbread's my favorite," she said.

"It's my favorite too," said Mormor. "If they behave themselves, maybe Björn and Bartholomew can lick the spoon."